COOKING WITH
CHEESE

Valerie Ferguson

LORENZ BOOKS

Contents

Introduction   4

Types of Cheese   6

Techniques   9

Soups & Starters   10

Simple Main Courses   20

Dinner Party Dishes   34

Desserts & Baking   52

Index   64

Introduction

Around the world, people of all ages enjoy cheese. It is a pleasure to eat on its own, with crackers or fresh fruit and it is a wonderfully versatile ingredient in cooked dishes. It goes well with leafy green vegetables, such as leeks and spinach, and has a natural affinity with eggs.

Cheese is packed with protein and is an excellent source of calcium. Some types have rather a high fat content, but there is an increasing number of reduced-fat varieties available. Remember, too, that soft cheese is generally lower in fat than hard and semi-hard. It is now also possible to buy a vegetarian version of many popular cheeses.

Cheese may be made from cow's, sheep's or goat's milk, pasteurized or unpasteurized, full-fat, skimmed or semi-skimmed. The variety is immense and the recipes in this book explore the particular qualities and characteristics of many familiar and some lesser-known cheeses. Sometimes cheese takes the starring role — most of all in Swiss Fondue — while at others it provides the finishing touch as a topping, sauce or flavoured butter.

Whether your choice is for mild or strongly flavoured cheese, you are sure to find a recipe to match.

Types of Cheese

There are many different types of cheese are available, which can be divided into hard, semi-hard, soft and blue. Some kinds of cheese are less suited to cooking than others.

Hard Cheeses

Cheddar has a close texture and a colour that ranges from pale honey to a deep orange or gold. Depending on its maturity, the flavour can be mild or sharp and nutty. Cheddar is excellent for cooking as it melts without becoming stringy. Red

Cheddar

Leicester is a strong-flavoured hard English cheese which is also very good for cooking.

Red Leicester

Blue Cheeses

Roquefort is a famous French crumbly blue-veined cheese traditionally made from ewe's milk. It tastes best when it is fully mature. Another very popular French blue cheese is the sharp tasting Fourme d'Ambert. Stilton is made only in Leicestershire and Derbyshire and is

Roquefort

considered the king of English cheeses. Blue Stilton is more mature and stronger than white. You can also buy Stilton with more unusual ingredients, such as apricots. Shropshire Blue, a firm red cheese, is milder tasting. Gorgonzola is a soft-textured

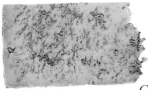

Fourme d'Ambert

Gorgonzola

blue cheese from Italy. The flavour ranges from mild to very sharp (Gorgonzola piccante). Try to track down mountain Gorgonzola which has a superior flavour. It is excellent sprinkled over pizza, and makes a wonderful base for a rich, cheesey pasta sauce. Dolcelatte is another Italian blue-veined cheese, and has a creamy texture and a delicate flavour.

Dolcelatte

French Soft Cheeses

Brie is a smooth creamy cheese made from cow's milk.
The white, floury crust is edible. Look for plump, soft, but not runny cheese.

Brie

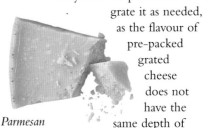

Camembert, a famous soft cheese made from cow's milk, has been made in Normandy for many centuries.

Camembert

Swiss Cheeses

Emmenthal is a wonderful cooking cheese. It is sweet and nutty, with distinctive grape-size holes.
Gruyère is moister than Emmenthal, which it resembles, and has a full, fruity flavour.

Emmenthal

It retains its flavour when cooked and is perhaps most famously used in fondues. The French cheese Beaufort is similar to Gruyère. Raclette is a semi-hard cheese traditionally melted and served with vegetables.

Gruyère

Italian Cheeses

Parmesan is Italy's gift to the cook and has a wonderfully distinctive flavour. Buy it in the piece and grate it as needed, as the flavour of pre-packed grated cheese does not have the same depth of flavour. Save the rind to use in soups to add extra flavour.

Parmesan

Fontina is a golden yellow cheese with tiny holes and a delicate, nutty flavour. It is perfect for fondues and other types of cooking. Mozzarella is a moist, delicately flavoured soft cheese made from cow's or water buffalo's milk.

Mozzarella

A fresh, full fat whey cheese, Ricotta has a mild, slightly sweet flavour. It is often used in desserts and makes an excellent cheesecake.

Ricotta

Mascarpone is a creamy full-fat soft cheese that is often used in desserts or served solo with fresh fruit. Mixed with natural (plain) yogurt, it makes a very good lighter alternative to whipped cream.

Dutch Cheeses

The well-known Edam is a milk-flavoured cheese with a red rind and is good for grating. Gouda has a shiny yellow rind with a few holes. Mature Gouda also grates well.

Edam

Ewe's and Goat's Milk Cheeses

The generic term for goat's milk cheeses is chèvre. The texture varies from soft and moist to hard and dry and the taste is usually quite tart. Soft varieties of goat's milk cheeses are usually moulded in cones or rolls. Feta is a Greek cheese, traditionally made from ewe's milk. The lightly pressed curds have a fresh, tangy flavour. Feta is frequently stored in brine to keep it moist. Halloumi is another Greek ewe's milk cheese. Semi-hard, it is excellent for grilling, but must be eaten while hot. Manchego was originally

Goat's cheese roll

Goat's cheese

Feta

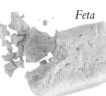

made in La Mancha but is now produced throughout Spain. It is a firm ewe's milk cheese with a nutty flavour. Pecorino is an Italian ewe's milk cheese which becomes stronger in flavour as it matures.

Pecorino

Curd Cheese

Made by separating the curds from the whey of cow's milk, this soft cheese is then drained and salted. It has a slightly tart flavour and is good for sweet and savoury dishes.

Smoked Cheeses

There are smoked versions of a number of popular cheeses, such as Cheddar and Mozzarella. Smoked Mozzarella is firmer and more complex in flavour. The technique of oak smoking gives the cheese a strong woody flavour and aroma. Their distinctive taste is excellent in baked pasta such as lasagne.

Oak-smoked Cheddar

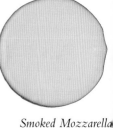

Smoked Mozzarella

Techniques

Grating

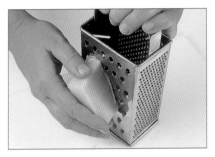

Choose a metal grater with a variety of surfaces with holes of different sizes. Square, triangular or hexagonal graters are easy to use, especially if there is a handle to prevent you from grating your fingers. Always use a firm, even pressure when grating cheese.

Slicing

Some cheeses, such as Mozzarella, Roquefort and Stilton, are better sliced than grated. Use a knife with a sharp, wide blade and don't make the slices too thin. You can also use a sharp vegetable peeler to cut slices of hard and smoked cheeses in narrow strips, if you prefer.

Melting

The secret of melting cheese is to use a low temperature. Too high a heat may cause it to curdle, separating into a blob of stringy curd surrounded by fat. It helps if you can melt the cheese with a liquid, such as wine or beer, but even then, the heat should be low and the pan should be removed as soon as the cheese has melted. Remove the pan from the heat, too, when adding grated cheese to a hot sauce, such as white sauce, and avoid reheating it.

Good cheeses for melting include Cheddar and Gruyère. Halloumi is a good toasting cheese, while fresh Parmesan makes a beautiful topping when melted on a gratin or pizza. You can also mix grated cheese with breadcrumbs.

Storing

Although cheeses are best bought in small quantities for immediate consumption, those containing over 45 per cent fat can be frozen. Wrap carefully and thaw well before using for cooking or eating straightaway.

Bread & Cheese Soup

It is worth using a good-quality Gorgonzola, farmhouse Cheddar or mature Gouda for this simple soup.

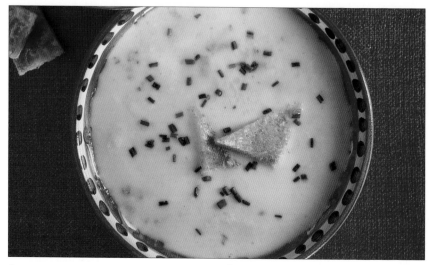

Serves 4

INGREDIENTS
115 g/4 oz strong-flavoured or blue cheese,
  or 175 g/6 oz mild cheese
600 ml/1 pint/2½ cups semi-skimmed milk
ground mace
4–6 slices stale bread, crusts removed
30 ml/2 tbsp olive oil
1 large garlic clove, crushed
salt and freshly ground black pepper
15 ml/1 tbsp snipped chives, to garnish

1 Remove any rinds from the cheese and grate into a heavy-based, preferably non-stick pan. Add the milk and heat through very slowly, stirring frequently to make sure it does not stick and burn.

2 When all the cheese has melted, add the ground mace and salt and freshly ground black pepper to taste, followed by one piece of bread. Cook over a very gentle heat until the bread has softened and slightly thickened the soup.

3 Mix the oil with the crushed garlic and brush over the remaining bread. Toast the bread until crisp, then cut the toast into triangles or fingers. Sprinkle the soup with the snipped chives and serve with the toast.

COOK'S TIP: Don't mix blue cheeses with other kinds of cheese in this soup.

Squash & Gruyère Soup

A lightly spiced squash soup, enriched with creamy melting cheese.

Serves 4

INGREDIENTS

900 g/2 lb butternut squash
   or pumpkin
15 ml/1 tbsp vegetable oil
225 g/8 oz onions, roughly chopped
2 garlic cloves, crushed
225 g/8 oz smoked back bacon, diced
10 ml/2 tsp ground cumin
15 ml/1 tbsp ground coriander
900 ml/1½ pints/3¾ cups vegetable stock
275 g/10 oz potatoes, peeled and cut into
   small chunks
10 ml/2 tsp cornflour (cornstarch)
30 ml/2 tbsp water
30 ml/2 tbsp crème fraîche
Tabasco sauce, to taste
175 g/6 oz/1½ cups grated Gruyère
salt and freshly ground black pepper

1 Cut the squash or pumpkin into pieces. Remove the skin. Scoop out the seeds. Chop the flesh into chunks.

2 Heat the oil in a saucepan and cook the onions and garlic for 3 minutes, or until beginning to soften. Add the bacon and cook for about 3 minutes. Add the spices and cook for 1 minute.

3 Add the squash or pumpkin, stock and potatoes. Simmer for 15 minutes, or until the vegetables are tender.

4 Blend the cornflour with the water and add with the crème fraîche. Bring to the boil and simmer, uncovered, for 3 minutes. Adjust the seasoning and add Tabasco sauce to taste. Serve in warm bowls, sprinkled with cheese.

Grilled Brie with Walnuts

This classic cheese starter will impress your dinner party guests, and requires almost no advance preparation.

Serves about 16–20

INGREDIENTS
15 g/½ oz/1 tbsp butter, at room temperature
5 ml/1 tsp Dijon mustard
675 g/1½ lb wheel of Brie
  or Camembert
25 g/1 oz/¼ cup chopped walnuts
French bread, sliced and toasted, to serve

1 Preheat the grill (broiler). In a bowl, cream together the butter and mustard, and spread evenly over the surface of the cheese. Transfer to a flameproof serving plate and grill (broil) 10–15 cm/ 4–6 in from the heat, for 3–4 minutes, until the top just begins to bubble.

2 Sprinkle the surface of the cheese with the chopped walnuts and place under the grill for 2–3 minutes longer, until the nuts are golden brown. Serve immediately with the French bread toasts. Allow your guests to help themselves as the whole brie makes an attractive centrepiece.

Cheese-stuffed Pears

These pears, with their scrumptious creamy mixed cheese topping, make a sublime dish when served with a simple salad.

Serves 4

INGREDIENTS
50 g/2 oz/¼ cup Ricotta cheese
50 g/2 oz/¼ cup Dolcelatte cheese
15 ml/1 tbsp honey
½ celery stick, finely sliced
8 green olives, stoned (pitted) and chopped
4 dates, stoned (pitted) and cut into strips
pinch of paprika
4 ripe pears
150 ml/¼ pint/⅔ cup apple juice

1 Preheat the oven to 200°C/400°F/ Gas 6. Place the Ricotta in a bowl and crumble in the Dolcelatte. Add the rest of the ingredients, except for the pears and apple juice, and mix well.

2 Halve the pears lengthways and use a melon baller to remove the cores. Place in an ovenproof dish and divide the filling equally among them.

3 Pour in the apple juice and cover the dish with foil. Bake the pears for 20 minutes, or until tender.

4 Remove the foil and place the dish under a hot grill (broiler) for 3 minutes. Serve the pears immediately.

COOK'S TIP: Choose ripe pears in season, such as Conference, William or Comice.

13

Potted Stilton

Make this cheese-filled pâté the day before and serve it in small ramekins, with the crisp Melba toast, as a snack or first course.

Serves 8

INGREDIENTS

225 g/8 oz blue Stilton or other blue cheese
115 g/4 oz cream cheese
15 ml/1 tbsp port
15 ml/1 tbsp chopped fresh parsley
15 ml/1 tbsp snipped fresh chives, plus extra
   to garnish
50 g/2 oz/½ cup finely chopped walnuts
12 thin slices white bread
salt and freshly ground black pepper

1 Put the Stilton, cream cheese and port into a food processor and process until smooth. Alternatively, beat together in a bowl.

2 Stir in the parsley, chives and walnuts and season with salt and pepper to taste.

3 Spoon into ramekins and level the tops. Cover with clear film and chill until firm. Sprinkle with snipped fresh chives before serving. To make the Melba toast, preheat the oven to 180°C/350°F/Gas 4. Toast the bread on both sides.

4 While still hot, cut off the crusts and cut each slice horizontally in two. Place in a single layer on baking trays and bake for 10–15 minutes, until golden brown and crisp.

Mediterranean Vegetables with Halloumi

Do not grill the Halloumi in advance or it will go rubbery.

Serves 4

INGREDIENTS
2 (bell) peppers, seeded and quartered
2 courgettes (zucchini), halved lengthways
2 small aubergines (eggplant), halved
  lengthways
1 fennel bulb, quartered
olive oil
115 g/4 oz Greek Halloumi cheese, sliced
salt and freshly ground black pepper

FOR THE TAHINI CREAM
225 g/8 oz/1 cup tahini paste
1 garlic clove, crushed
30 ml/2 tbsp olive oil
30 ml/2 tbsp fresh lemon juice
120 ml/4 fl oz/½ cup cold water

1 Preheat the grill (broiler) or barbecue until hot. Brush the vegetables with the oil and grill (broil) until just browned, turning once.

2 Place the vegetables in a shallow dish and season. Allow to cool. Brush the cheese slices with oil and grill on both sides until just charred. Remove and add to the vegetables.

3 To make the tahini cream, place all the ingredients, except the water, in a food processor. Process for a few seconds, then, with the motor still running, pour in the water and process until smooth. Serve trickled over the vegetables and cheese.

15

Artichoke Rice Cakes with Manchego

If possible, use *Manchego en aciete*, which has been matured in olive oil and has a superbly rich flavour.

Serves 6

INGREDIENTS
1 globe artichoke
50 g/2 oz/¼ cup butter
1 small onion, finely chopped
1 garlic clove, finely chopped
115 g/4 oz/⅔ cup risotto rice
450 ml/¾ pint/scant 2 cups
    hot chicken stock
50 g/2 oz/¼ cup grated
    Parmesan cheese
150 g/5 oz Manchego cheese,
    very finely diced
45–60 ml/3–4 tbsp fine cornmeal
olive oil, for frying
salt and freshly ground
    black pepper
flat leaf parsley, to garnish

1 Remove the stalk, leaves and choke to leave just the heart of the artichoke; chop the heart finely.

2 Melt the butter in a saucepan and gently fry the artichoke heart, onion and garlic for 5 minutes, until softened. Stir in the rice and cook for about 1 minute.

3 Over a fairly high heat, gradually add the hot chicken stock, stirring constantly until all the liquid has been absorbed and the rice is cooked – this should take about 20 minutes. Season and stir in the grated Parmesan. Transfer the mixture to a bowl. Cool, then cover and chill for at least 2 hours.

4 Spoon about 15 ml/1 tbsp of the mixture into the palm of one hand, flatten slightly, and place a few pieces of diced Manchego cheese in the centre. Shape the rice around the cheese to make a small ball. Flatten slightly then roll in the cornmeal, shaking off any excess. Repeat with the remaining mixture to make about 12 cakes.

5 Shallow fry the rice cakes in hot olive oil for 4–5 minutes, until they are crisp and golden brown. Drain on kitchen paper and serve hot, garnished with flat leaf parsley.

COOK'S TIP: It is important that these rice cakes are served hot, while the Manchego is still creamy and melting.

Onion Tarts with Goat's Cheese

Mild, creamy fresh goat's cheese provides a perfect contrast to the sharpness of the onions in this classic tart.

Serves 8

INGREDIENTS
15–25 ml/1–1½ tbsp olive or
   sunflower oil
3 onions, finely sliced
175 g/6 oz fresh goat's cheese
2 eggs, beaten
15 ml/1 tbsp single (light) cream
50 g/2 oz/½ cup grated
   goat's Cheddar
15 ml/1 tbsp chopped fresh tarragon
salt and freshly ground
   black pepper

FOR THE PASTRY
175 g/6 oz/1½ cups plain (all-purpose)
   flour
65 g/2½ oz/5 tbsp butter
25 g/1 oz/¼ cup grated goat's Cheddar
   or Cheddar cheese

1 To make the pastry, sift the flour into a bowl and rub in the butter. Stir in the grated cheese and add enough cold water to make a dough. Knead lightly, cover and chill. Preheat the oven to 190°C/375°F/Gas 5.

2 Roll out the dough on a lightly floured surface, cut into eight rounds and line eight 10 cm/4 in patty tins.

3 Prick the bases with a fork and bake for 10–15 minutes, until firm but not browned. Reduce the oven temperature to 180°C/350°F/Gas 4.

4 Heat the olive oil or sunflower oil in a frying pan and fry the onions over a low heat for 20–25 minutes, until golden. Stir occasionally to prevent them burning.

5 Beat the goat's cheese with the eggs, cream, goat's Cheddar and chopped fresh tarragon. Season with salt and freshly ground black pepper and stir in the fried onions.

6 Pour the mixture into the part-baked pastry cases and bake the tarts for 20–25 minutes, until they are golden. Serve warm or cold.

Spicy Sausage & Cheese Tortilla

A colourful Spanish-style omelette, incorporating strong Cheddar cheese, which is delicious hot or cold, cut into wedges, with a tomato salad.

Serves 4–6

INGREDIENTS
675 g/1½ lb potatoes
275 g/10 oz onions
175 g/6 oz chorizo or spicy sausages
75 ml/5 tbsp olive oil
4 eggs, beaten
30 ml/2 tbsp chopped fresh parsley
115 g/4 oz/1 cup grated
   Cheddar cheese
salt and freshly ground
   black pepper
fresh flat leaf parsley, to garnish

1 Thinly slice the potatoes. Halve and thinly slice the onions. Thinly slice the chorizo or spicy sausages.

2 Heat 15 ml/1 tbsp of olive oil in a 20 cm/8 in non-stick frying pan and fry the sliced sausage until golden brown and cooked through. Drain on kitchen paper.

3 Add a further 30 ml/2 tbsp oil and fry the sliced potatoes and onions for 2–3 minutes, turning frequently (the pan will be very full). Cover tightly and cook over a gentle heat for about 30 minutes, turning occasionally, until softened and slightly golden.

4 Mix the beaten eggs in a large bowl, with the chopped fresh parsley, grated cheese, sausage and salt and freshly ground black pepper. Gently stir in the potatoes and onions until coated, taking care not to break up the potatoes too much.

5 Wipe out the pan with kitchen paper and heat the remaining 30 ml/ 2 tbsp oil. Add the mixture and cook over a low heat, until the egg begins to set. Use a palette knife to prevent the tortilla from sticking to the sides.

6 Preheat the grill (broiler) to hot. When the base has set, protect the pan handle with foil and place under the grill until set and golden. Turn out, garnish with flat leaf parsley and cut into wedges to serve.

Little Meatballs with Fontina

In this Italian dish, meatballs are filled with cubes of creamy Fontina cheese and then rolled in crumbs and fried.

Serves 6–8

INGREDIENTS

500 g/1¼ lb lean minced (ground) beef
500 g/1¼ lb lean minced (ground) pork
3 garlic cloves, crushed
grated rind and juice of 1 lemon
2 slices of day-old bread, crumbed
40 g/1½ oz/½ cup grated
   Parmesan cheese
2.5 ml/½ tsp ground cinnamon
5 ml/1 tsp dried oregano
2 eggs, beaten
5 ml/1 tsp salt
150 g/5 oz Fontina cheese,
   cut into 16 cubes
115–150 g/4–5 oz/1–1¼ cups natural-
   coloured dried breadcrumbs
olive oil, for frying
freshly ground black pepper
fresh basil and grated Parmesan cheese,
   to garnish
cooked pasta, a mixed leaf salad and
   tomato sauce, to serve

VARIATION: Cubes of Raclette or Gouda can be used instead of Fontina. Dip your hands in cold water occasionally during the kneading process.

1 Preheat the oven to 180°C/350°F/ Gas 4. Put the meat, garlic, lemon rind and juice, breadcrumbs, Parmesan, cinnamon and oregano in a bowl. Stir in the beaten eggs and beat well. Add the salt and pepper to taste.

2 Knead the mixture well, then shape it into 16 balls. Cup each ball in your hand and press a piece of Fontina into the centre. Reshape the ball, making sure the cheese is well covered.

3 Roll the meatballs in the dried crumbs. Heat the olive oil in a large frying pan. Add the meatballs in batches and cook until lightly browned and sealed.

4 Transfer them to a roasting tin and bake for 20 minutes, or until cooked through. Garnish with fresh basil and Parmesan and serve with pasta, salad and tomato sauce.

Wild Mushroom Gratin with Beaufort Cheese

This Swiss-inspired gratin combines a distinctively flavoured cheese with both wild and cultivated mushrooms.

Serves 4

INGREDIENTS

900 g/2 lb new potatoes, scrubbed or scraped
50 g/2 oz/4 tbsp unsalted butter or 60 ml/
   4 tbsp olive oil, plus a knob of butter
350 g/12 oz assorted wild and cultivated
   mushrooms, thinly sliced
175 g/6 oz Beaufort or Fontina cheese
50 g/2 oz/½ cup broken walnuts, toasted
salt and freshly ground black pepper
12 medium gherkins and mixed green salad
   leaves, to serve

2 Fry the wild and cultivated mushrooms in the unsalted butter or the oil. When the mushroom juices appear, increase the heat to evaporate the moisture.

1 Place the potatoes in a pan of salted water, bring to the boil and cook for 20 minutes. Drain, add the knob of butter, cover and keep warm.

COOK'S TIP: Choose an attractive flameproof dish that can be brought directly to the table.

3 Preheat a moderate grill (broiler). Slice the cheese thinly, arrange on top of the mushroom slices and grill (broil) until bubbly and brown.

4 Scatter with toasted walnuts and serve with buttered new potatoes, gherkins and a green salad.

Tagliatelle with Gorgonzola Sauce

The piquancy and rich flavour of Gorgonzola is unique, but you could use Danish Blue as an alternative.

Serves 4

INGREDIENTS
25 g/1 oz/2 tbsp butter,
   plus extra for tossing
   the pasta
225 g/8 oz Gorgonzola
150 ml/¼ pint/⅔ cup double or
   whipping cream
30 ml/2 tbsp dry vermouth
5 ml/1 tsp cornflour (cornstarch)
15 ml/1 tbsp chopped
   fresh sage
450 g/1 lb dried tagliatelle
salt and freshly ground black pepper

1 Melt the butter in a heavy-based saucepan. Stir in 175 g/6 oz/¾ cup crumbled Gorgonzola and stir the mixture continuously over a very gentle heat for 2–3 minutes, until the cheese has melted.

2 Pour in the cream, vermouth and cornflour, whisking well to amalgamate. Stir in the sage and season to taste. Cook, whisking all the time, until the sauce boils and thickens. Set aside.

3 Cook the pasta in plenty of boiling salted water for 8–10 minutes, until tender, but still firm to the bite. Drain well and toss with a little butter.

4 Reheat the sauce gently, whisking well. Divide the pasta among four bowls, top with sauce, sprinkle over the remaining cheese and serve.

Baked Leeks with Cheese & Yogurt Topping

You can use either mild fresh or tangy mature goat's cheese, as both combine well with the fragrant flavour of Parmesan.

Serves 4

INGREDIENTS
8 small leeks, about 675 g/1½ lb
2 small eggs or 1 large one, beaten
150 g/5 oz fresh goat's cheese
75 ml/5 tbsp natural (plain) yogurt
50 g/2 oz/⅔ cup grated
    Parmesan cheese
25 g/1 oz/½ cup fresh white or
    brown breadcrumbs

1 Preheat the oven to 180°C/350°F/ Gas 4 and butter a shallow ovenproof dish. Trim the leeks, cut a slit from top to bottom and rinse well between the layers under cold water.

2 Place the leeks in a saucepan of water, bring to the boil and simmer gently for 6–8 minutes, until the leeks are just tender. Remove from the water, drain well and arrange in the prepared ovenproof dish.

3 Beat the eggs with the goat's cheese, yogurt and half the Parmesan and season well with salt and pepper.

4 Pour the cheese and yogurt mixture over the leeks. Mix the breadcrumbs and remaining Parmesan together and sprinkle over the sauce. Bake in the oven for 35–40 minutes, until the top is crisp and golden brown.

COOK'S TIP: Small, young leeks, available at the start of the season, are ideal for this dish.

Gorgonzola & Cauliflower Gratin

This cauliflower dish is covered with a strong blue cheese sauce and cooked under the grill until bubbling.

Serves 4

INGREDIENTS
1 large cauliflower,
    broken into florets
25 g/1 oz/2 tbsp butter
1 medium onion, finely chopped
45 ml/3 tbsp plain (all-purpose) flour
450 ml/¾ pint/scant 2 cups milk
150 g/5 oz Gorgonzola or other
    blue cheese, cut into pieces
2.5 ml/½ tsp celery salt
pinch of cayenne pepper
fresh parsley, to garnish
green salad, to serve

1 Bring a large saucepan of salted water to the boil and cook the cauliflower for 6 minutes. Drain and place in a gratin dish.

2 Heat the butter in a heavy-based saucepan. Add the onion and cook over a gentle heat until softened. Stir in the flour, then remove from the heat. Gradually stir in the milk. Add the cheese, celery salt and cayenne pepper. Simmer and stir to thicken.

3 Preheat a moderate grill (broiler). Spoon the sauce over the cauliflower and grill (broil) until golden. Garnish with parsley and serve with salad.

Pizza with Four Cheeses

Any combination of fresh or smoked cheeses can be used, but choose cheeses that are different in character.

Serves 4

INGREDIENTS
1 ready-made pizza base
75 g/3 oz Gorgonzola or other blue cheese, thinly sliced
75 g/3 oz/¾ cup finely diced smoked Mozzarella cheese
75 g/3 oz goat's cheese, thinly sliced
75 g/3 oz/¾ cup coarsely grated mature (aged) Cheddar cheese
4 leaves fresh sage, torn into pieces, or 45 ml/3 tbsp chopped fresh parsley
salt and freshly ground black pepper
45 ml/3 tbsp olive oil

1 Preheat the oven to 240°C/475°F/Gas 9. Arrange the Gorgonzola on one quarter of the pizza and the Mozzarella on another, leaving the edge free.

2 Arrange the sliced goat's and grated Cheddar cheeses on the remaining two quarters.

3 Sprinkle with the herbs, salt and pepper and olive oil. Immediately place the pizza in the oven. Bake for 15–20 minutes, or until the crust is golden brown and the cheeses are melted and bubbling.

Polenta Baked with Cheese

In this Italian recipe, cold polenta is cut into slices and baked in layers with cheese and other ingredients.

Serves 4–6

INGREDIENTS
250 g/9 oz/2 cups polenta flour
75 g/3 oz/6 tbsp butter
45 ml/3 tbsp olive oil
2 medium onions, thinly sliced
pinch of grated nutmeg
150 g/5 oz Mozzarella or mature (aged)
   Cheddar cheese, cut into
   thin slices
45 ml/3 tbsp finely chopped
   fresh parsley
40 g/1½ oz/⅓ cup grated
   Parmesan cheese
salt and freshly ground black pepper

1 Cook the polenta according to the packet instructions. Stir a third of the butter into the cooked polenta.

2 Sprinkle a work surface with a little water. Spread the polenta out on to the surface in a layer 1 cm/½ in thick. Allow to cool. Cut the polenta into 6 cm/2½ in rounds.

3 Heat the olive oil in a medium saucepan with 15 g/½ oz/1 tbsp of the remaining butter. Add the sliced onions, and stir over a low heat until the onions are soft.

4 Season the onions with the grated nutmeg, salt and freshly ground black pepper. Preheat the oven to 190°C/375°F/Gas 5. Butter an ovenproof dish. Spread a few of the onion slices in the base of the dish. Cover the onion with a layer of the polenta rounds. Dot the polenta with butter.

5 Add a layer of the sliced Mozzarella or Cheddar and a sprinkling of parsley and Parmesan. Season with salt and pepper. Make another layer of the onions and continue the layers in order, ending with the Parmesan. Dot the top with butter.

6 Bake the polenta in the oven for 20–25 minutes, or until the cheese has melted. Serve immediately.

VARIATION: Freshly chopped herbs could be added to the cooked polenta.

Cannelloni with Tuna

Fontina cheese has a sweet, nutty flavour and very good melting qualities. Look for it in large supermarkets and Italian delicatessens.

Serves 4–6

INGREDIENTS
50 g/2 oz/¼ cup butter
50 g/2 oz/½ cup plain (all-purpose) flour
about 900 ml/1½ pints/3¾ cups
    hot milk
2 x 200 g/7 oz cans tuna, drained
115 g/4 oz/1 cup grated
    Fontina cheese
1.5 ml/¼ tsp grated nutmeg
12 no-precook cannelloni tubes
50 g/2 oz/⅔ cup grated
    Parmesan cheese
salt and freshly ground black pepper
fresh herbs, to garnish

2 Mix the tuna with about 120 ml/ 4 fl oz/½ cup of the warm white sauce in a bowl. Season to taste with salt and pepper. Preheat the oven to 180°C/ 350°F/Gas 4.

3 Gradually whisk the remaining milk into the rest of the sauce, then return to the heat and simmer, whisking constantly, until thickened. Add the Fontina and nutmeg, with salt and pepper to taste. Simmer for a few more minutes, stirring frequently.

1 Melt the butter in a heavy-based saucepan, add the flour and stir over a low heat for 1–2 minutes. Remove from the heat and gradually add 350 ml/12 fl oz/1½ cups of the milk, beating vigorously. Return the pan to the heat and whisk for 1–2 minutes, until the sauce is very thick and smooth. Remove from the heat.

4 Pour about one-third of the sauce into an ovenproof dish and spread to the corners.

5 Fill the cannelloni with the tuna mixture, pushing it in with the handle of a teaspoon. Place in a single layer in the dish. Thin the remaining sauce with more milk, if necessary, then pour over the cannelloni. Sprinkle with Parmesan and bake for 30 minutes, or until golden. Serve hot, garnished with herbs.

35

Haddock with Gruyère and Leek Sauté

Instead of the classic cheese sauce this Gruyère topped leek sauté allows the fresh taste of the haddock fillet to dominate.

Serves 4

INGREDIENTS
4 x 225 g/8 oz haddock fillets
675 g/1½ lb leeks
1 onion
50 g/2 oz/4 tbsp butter
5 ml/1 tsp caraway seeds
50 g/2 oz/½ cup finely
    grated Gruyère
salt and freshly ground
    black pepper
strands of fresh chives,
    to garnish

2 Slice the leeks and rinse the slices thoroughly in plenty of cold water. Drain the leek slices well. Cut the onion in half lengthways and thinly slice into half rings.

1 Remove any remaining bones from the haddock using tweezers. Rinse under cold water and pat dry with kitchen paper. Season with salt and freshly ground black pepper. Preheat the grill (broiler) to medium.

3 Heat the butter in a large heavy-based saucepan and gently sauté the sliced leeks and onion until they are soft but not brown. This will take about 8 minutes. Stir in the caraway seeds and cook for 1 minute until the aroma of the spice is released.

4 Line the base of a shallow ovenproof dish with the vegetable mixture. Sprinkle over the cheese and top with the haddock fillets. Grill (broil) for 10 minutes, until cooked. Serve hot, garnished with the chives.

VARIATION: This recipe works equally well with other types of white fish, such as cod or plaice.

Parmesan Chicken Bake

Layers of chicken, Mozzarella and Parmesan cheese, smothered in home-made tomato sauce, will simply melt in the mouth.

Serves 4

INGREDIENTS
4 skinless, boneless chicken breasts
60 ml/4 tbsp plain (all-purpose) flour
60 ml/4 tbsp olive oil
225 g/8 oz Mozzarella cheese, sliced
60 ml/4 tbsp grated Parmesan cheese
30 ml/2 tbsp fresh breadcrumbs
salt and freshly ground black pepper

FOR THE TOMATO SAUCE
15 ml/1 tbsp olive oil
1 onion, finely chopped
1 stick celery, finely chopped
1 red (bell) pepper, seeded and diced
1 garlic clove, crushed
400 g/14 oz can chopped tomatoes
150 ml/¼ pint/⅔ cup chicken stock
15 ml/1 tbsp tomato purée (paste)
10 ml/2 tsp caster (superfine) sugar
15 ml/1 tbsp chopped fresh
   basil, plus a whole sprig, to garnish
15 ml/1 tbsp chopped fresh parsley

1 First make the tomato sauce. Heat 15 ml/1 tbsp of the olive oil in a frying pan and cook the onion, celery, pepper and garlic over a low heat until all the vegetables are tender.

2 Add the tomatoes with their juice, the chicken stock, tomato purée, sugar, and the fresh basil and parsley. Season to taste and bring to the boil. Simmer the mixture, stirring occasionally, for 30 minutes, until thick.

3 Divide each of the chicken breasts into two fillets, place them between sheets of clear film and flatten to a thickness of 5 mm/¼ in by pressing down firmly with a rolling pin.

4 Season the flour with salt and freshly ground black pepper. Toss the chicken breasts in the flour to coat, shaking to remove the excess.

5 Preheat the oven to 180°C/350°F/ Gas 4. Heat the remaining oil in a large frying pan and cook the chicken quickly, in batches, for 3–4 minutes, until coloured. Keep each batch warm while you fry the rest.

6 Layer the chicken pieces with the cheeses and thick tomato sauce, finishing with a layer of Parmesan and breadcrumbs on top. Bake uncovered for 20–30 minutes, or until golden brown. Garnish with fresh basil.

Chicken Cordon Bleu

This perennially popular classic consists of chicken breasts stuffed with slices of smoked ham and Gruyère, coated in egg and fine breadcrumbs and then lightly fried until golden.

Serves 4

INGREDIENTS
4 skinless, boneless chicken breasts,
    about 130 g/4½ oz each
4 very thin smoked ham slices,
    halved and rind removed
about 90 g/3½ oz Gruyère,
    thinly sliced
plain (all-purpose) flour, for coating
2 eggs, beaten
75 g/3 oz/¾ cup natural-coloured
    dried breadcrumbs
5 ml/1 tsp dried thyme
40 g/1½ oz/3 tbsp butter
30 ml/2 tbsp olive oil
salt and freshly ground
    black pepper
mixed leaf salad, to serve

1 Slit the chicken breasts about three-quarters of the way through, open them up and lay them flat. Place a slice of ham on each cut side of the chicken, trimming to fit if necessary.

2 Top the ham slices with the Gruyère slices, making sure that they are within the edges of the ham slices. Fold over the chicken and reshape, pressing well to seal.

3 Put the flour into a bowl. Pour the eggs into another bowl and mix the breadcrumbs with the thyme and seasoning in a third bowl.

4 Toss each stuffed breast in the flour, then coat in egg and breadcrumbs, shaking off any excess. Lay the crumbed breasts flat on a plate, cover and chill for at least 1 hour.

5 Heat the butter and olive oil in a large frying pan. Gently slide in the coated chicken breasts, two at a time. Fry over a medium-low heat for about 5 minutes each side, turning over carefully with a fish slice. Drain the chicken on kitchen paper and keep hot. Serve with a mixed leaf side salad.

Rump Steak with Roquefort & Walnut Butter

The strongly-flavoured Roquefort in this savoury butter makes it the ideal topping for a robust pan-fried steak.

Serves 4

INGREDIENTS
2 shallots, chopped
75 g/3 oz/6 tbsp butter,
   slightly softened
150 g/5 oz Roquefort cheese
30 ml/2 tbsp finely chopped walnuts
15 ml/1 tbsp finely snipped
   fresh chives
15 ml/1 tbsp olive oil or
   sunflower oil
4 lean rump steaks, about
   115 g/4 oz each
120 ml/4 fl oz/½ cup dry
   white wine
30 ml/2 tbsp crème fraîche or
   double (heavy) cream
salt and freshly ground
   black pepper
fresh chives, to garnish
green beans, to serve

COOK'S TIPS: For extra convenience, make up a roll of the savoury blue cheese butter in advance and keep it in the freezer for topping steaks. You might also like to try serving the butter as a topping for pork chops.

1 Sauté the shallots in a third of the butter. Tip into a bowl and add half the remaining butter, the cheese, walnuts, snipped chives and pepper to taste. Chill lightly, roll in foil to a sausage shape and chill again until firm.

2 Heat the remaining butter with the oil in a heavy-based frying pan and cook the steaks for about 3 minutes each side, or until cooked to your liking. Season the steaks and remove them from the pan.

3 Pour the wine into the pan and stir to incorporate any sediment. Boil for 1–2 minutes, then stir in the crème fraîche or cream. Season and pour over the steaks.

4 Cut pats of the Roquefort butter and put one on top of each steak. Garnish with chives. Serve immediately with lightly cooked green beans.

Classic Cheese Soufflé

At its simplest, a soufflé is merely a thick cheese sauce with beaten egg whites folded in – not at all difficult to achieve.

Serves 2–3

INGREDIENTS
50 g/2 oz/¼ cup butter
30–45 ml/2–3 tbsp natural-coloured
   dried breadcrumbs
200 ml/7 fl oz/scant 1 cup milk
30 g/1¼ oz/3 tbsp plain (all-purpose) flour
pinch of cayenne pepper
2.5 ml/½ tsp curry paste
   or mustard or freshly
   grated nutmeg
50 g/2 oz/½ cup grated mature
   Cheddar cheese
25 g/1 oz/⅓ cup grated
   Parmesan cheese
4 eggs, separated, plus 1 egg white
salt and freshly ground
   black pepper

1 Preheat the oven to 190°C/375°F/ Gas 5. Melt 15 ml/1 tbsp of the butter and use it to grease a 1.2 litre/2 pint/ 5 cup soufflé dish. Coat the inside of the soufflé dish evenly with the natural-coloured dried breadcrumbs.

2 Put the milk in a large saucepan. Add the remaining butter, flour and cayenne pepper, with the curry paste, mustard or grated nutmeg. Bring to the boil over a low heat, whisking steadily until the mixture thickens to make a smooth sauce.

3 Simmer the sauce for 1–2 minutes, then turn off the heat and whisk in all the grated Cheddar and half the Parmesan. Allow to cool a little, then beat in the egg yolks and taste the sauce to check the seasoning.

4 Whisk all the egg whites in a large grease-free bowl until they form soft, glossy peaks.

5 Spoon some of the beaten egg whites into the sauce to lighten it. Beat well, then scrape the rest of the whites into the pan and, using a figure-of-eight movement, carefully fold them into the mixture with a large metal spoon.

6 Pour into the dish, level the top and place on a baking sheet. Sprinkle on the remaining Parmesan. Bake for 20–25 minutes, until risen and golden. Serve immediately.

Swiss Fondue

This traditional dish is a mixture of melted cheeses with wine to keep it
liquid. Garlic and kirsch add extra flavour.

Serves 6

INGREDIENTS
1 large garlic clove, halved
5 ml/1 tsp arrowroot or
   potato starch
300 ml/½ pint/1¼ cups dry
   white wine
3 x 350 g/12 oz portions hard
   melting cheese, such as Emmenthal,
   Gouda, Gruyère or Raclette,
   thinly sliced or
   coarsely grated
45–60 ml/3–4 tbsp kirsch
freshly ground black pepper
cubes of country-style bread,
   for dipping

1 Rub the inside of a *caquelon*
(traditional fondue pan) or deep
flameproof pan with the cut side of
the garlic halves. If you like, you can
then chop the garlic finely and place it
in the pan.

COOK'S TIPS: The arrowroot or
potato starch used in this recipe
prevents the cheeses from separating.
   It is important that the fondue
stays piping hot at the table, but
watch it carefully, as it must not be
allowed to boil.
   If possible, use special long-
handled fondue forks for spearing.

2 Mix the arrowroot or potato starch
with 30 ml/2 tbsp of the dry white
wine in a small bowl. Set aside until
needed. Pour the rest of the wine into
the *caquelon* or pan.

3 Heat the wine over a very low
heat. Add about a third of the sliced or
grated cheese, and continue slowly
heating the mixture, stirring constantly
until the cheese starts to melt and the
liquid starts to bubble.

4 Slowly stir in the arrowroot or
potato starch mixture, followed by the
rest of the cheese, a little at a time. Add
the kirsch and freshly ground black
pepper. Place the fondue over a candle
warmer on the table, accompanied
by cubes of country-style bread,
for dipping.

VARIATION: If you prefer, rum
may be substituted for the kirsch in
this recipe.

Risotto with Four Cheeses

This is a very rich dish combining the flavours of different cheeses.
Serve it for a dinner party with chilled sparkling white wine to drink.

Serves 6

INGREDIENTS
40 g/1½ oz/3 tbsp butter
1 small onion, finely chopped
1 litre/1¾ pints/4 cups boiling
    chicken stock
350 g/12 oz/1¼ cups risotto rice
200 ml/7 fl oz/scant 1 cup sparkling
    dry white wine
50 g/2 oz/½ cup grated Gruyère
50 g/2 oz/½ cup diced Fontina cheese
50 g/2 oz/½ cup crumbled Gorgonzola
50 g/2 oz/⅔ cup freshly grated Parmesan
salt and freshly ground black pepper
fresh flat leaf parsley, to garnish

1 Melt the butter in a saucepan until
foaming. Add the onion and cook
gently, stirring frequently, for about
3 minutes, until softened. Have the
hot stock ready in an adjacent pan.

COOK'S TIP: It is important to use
risotto rice, such as arborio or
carnaroli, for this dish, rather than
substituting it with long grain rice.

2 Add the rice to the pan containing
the onion and stir until the grains start
to swell and burst, then add the
sparkling wine. Stir until it stops
sizzling and most of it has been
absorbed by the rice, then pour in a
little of the hot stock. Add salt and
pepper to taste. Stir over a low heat
until the stock has been absorbed.

3 Add more stock, a little at a time,
allowing the rice to absorb it before
adding more, and stirring constantly.
After 20–25 minutes the rice will be
tender and the risotto creamy.

VARIATION: If you're feeling
especially extravagant you can use
Champagne as the sparkling wine in
this risotto, although Asti Spumante
works perfectly well and is more
often used.

4 Turn off the heat under the pan, then add the Gruyère, Fontina, Gorgonzola and 30 ml/2 tbsp of the Parmesan. Stir gently until the cheeses have melted, then taste for seasoning. Tip the risotto into a serving bowl and garnish with the fresh flat leaf parsley. Hand round the remaining Parmesan separately.

Spinach in Filo with Three Cheeses

With its combination of creamy and tasty cheeses this dish makes a good choice to serve when vegetarians and meat eaters are gathered for a meal.

Serves 4

INGREDIENTS
450 g/1 lb spinach
15 ml/1 tbsp sunflower oil
15 g/½ oz/1 tbsp butter
1 small onion, finely chopped
175 g/6 oz/¾ cup Ricotta cheese
115 g/4 oz/1 cup diced Feta cheese
75 g/3 oz/¾ cup grated Gruyère
    or Emmenthal cheese
15 ml/1 tbsp chopped
    fresh chervil
5 ml/1 tsp chopped fresh marjoram
5 large or 10 small sheets
    filo pastry
40–50 g/1½–2 oz/3–4 tbsp
    butter, melted
salt and freshly ground black pepper

1 Preheat the oven to 190°C/375°F/ Gas 5. Cook the spinach in a large saucepan over a moderate heat, shaking the pan occasionally, for 3–4 minutes, until the leaves have wilted. Strain and press out the excess liquid.

2 Heat the oil and butter in a saucepan and fry the chopped onion for 3–4 minutes, until softened. Remove from the heat and add half the spinach. Combine, using a metal spoon to break up the spinach.

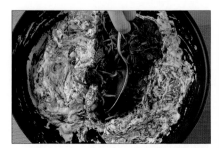

3 Add the Ricotta cheese and stir until evenly combined. Stir in the remaining spinach, again chopping it into the mixture with a metal spoon. Fold in the Feta and Gruyère or Emmenthal cheese, chervil, marjoram and seasoning.

4 Lay a sheet of filo pastry measuring about 30 cm/12 in square on a work surface. (If you have small filo sheets, lay them side by side, overlapping by about 2.5 cm/1 in in the middle.) Brush with melted butter and cover with a second sheet; brush with butter and build up five layers in this way.

5 Spread the cheese and spinach filling over the filo pastry layers, leaving a 2.5 cm/1 in border all around. Fold the sides of the pastry inwards and then carefully roll up.

6 Place the roll, seam side down, on a greased baking sheet and brush with the remaining butter. Bake in the oven for about 30 minutes, until crisp and golden brown.

Lemon & Lime Cheesecake

Tangy lemon cheesecakes are always a hit and are easy to make. The lime syrup makes this a citrus sensation.

Serves 8

INGREDIENTS
150 g/5 oz digestive biscuits (graham crackers)
40 g/1½ oz/3 tbsp butter

FOR THE TOPPING
grated rind (zest) and juice of 2 lemons
10 ml/2 tsp powdered gelatine
250 g/9 oz/generous 1 cup
    Ricotta cheese
75 g/3 oz/⅓ cup caster (superfine) sugar
100 ml/3 fl oz/⅓ cup double (heavy) cream
2 eggs, separated

FOR THE LIME SYRUP
finely pared rind (zest) and juice of
    3 limes
75 g/3 oz/⅓ cup caster (superfine) sugar
5 ml/1 tsp arrowroot mixed with
    30 ml/2 tbsp water
a little green food
    colouring (optional)

1 Lightly grease a 20 cm/8 in round springform cake tin. Place the biscuits in a food processor or blender and process until they form fine crumbs.

2 Melt the butter in a large saucepan, then stir in the crumbs until well coated. Spoon into the prepared cake tin, press the crumbs down well in an even layer, then chill.

3 Make the topping. Place the lemon rind and juice in a small saucepan and sprinkle over the gelatine. Leave to soften for 5 minutes. Heat gently until the gelatine has melted, then set the mixture aside to cool slightly.

4 Beat the Ricotta cheese and sugar in a bowl. Stir in the double cream and the egg yolks, then whisk in the cooled lemon and gelatine mixture.

5 Whisk the egg whites in a grease-free bowl until they form soft peaks. Fold them into the cheese mixture. Spoon on to the biscuit base, level the surface and chill for 2–3 hours.

6 Meanwhile, make the lime syrup. Place the lime rind, juice and caster sugar in a small saucepan. Bring to the boil, stirring, then boil the syrup for 5 minutes. Stir in the arrowroot mixture and continue to stir until the syrup boils again and thickens slightly. Tint pale green with a little food colouring, if you like. Cool, then chill until required.

7 Spoon the lime syrup over the set cheesecake. Remove from the tin and cut into slices to serve.

> VARIATION: If you prefer, you can use gingernut biscuits (cookies) for the base instead of digestive. You might also like to sprinkle a little grated chocolate on top.

Cherry & Hazelnut Strudel

The Ricotta cheese in this recipe gives the strudel filling a creamy texture. Serve this wonderful old-world treat as a warm dessert with custard, or allow it to cool and offer it as a scrumptious cake with coffee.

Serves 6–8

INGREDIENTS
75 g/3 oz/6 tbsp butter
90 ml/6 tbsp light brown sugar
3 egg yolks
grated rind (zest) of 1 lemon
1.5 ml/¼ tsp grated nutmeg
250 g/9 oz/generous 1 cup
　Ricotta cheese
8 large sheets filo pastry,
　thawed if frozen
75 g/3 oz ratafias (sugar cookies), crushed
450 g/1 lb/2½ cups cherries, stoned
30 ml/2 tbsp chopped hazelnuts
icing (confectioners') sugar, for dusting
crème fraîche, to serve

1 Preheat the oven to 190°C/375°F/ Gas 5. Soften 15 g/½ oz/1 tbsp of the butter. Place it in a bowl and beat in the sugar and egg yolks until light and fluffy. Beat in the lemon rind, nutmeg and Ricotta, then set aside.

2 Melt the remaining butter in a small pan. Working quickly, place a sheet of filo on a clean dish towel and brush it generously with melted butter. Place a second sheet on top and repeat the process. Continue until all the filo has been layered and buttered, reserving some of the melted butter.

3 Scatter the crushed ratafias over the top, leaving a 5 cm/2 in border around the outside.

4 Spoon the Ricotta mixture over the biscuits, spread it lightly to cover, then scatter over the cherries.

5 Fold the filo pastry border over the Ricotta and cherry filling and use the dish towel to roll up the strudel gently, Swiss-roll style, beginning from one of the long sides of the pastry. Grease a baking sheet with the remaining melted butter.

6 Carefully place the strudel on the greased baking sheet, seam-side down, and scatter the chopped hazelnuts over the surface.

7 Bake in the oven for 35–40 minutes or until the strudel is golden brown and crisp. Dust with icing sugar and serve with crème fraîche.

Coeur à la Crème

This cheese dessert is sheer simplicity.

Serves 8

INGREDIENTS

250 g/9 oz/generous 1 cup cottage cheese
300 ml/½ pint/1¼ cups crème fraîche or
    natural (plain) yogurt
30–45 ml/2–3 tbsp vanilla-flavoured
    caster (superfine) sugar
raspberry leaves, to decorate

FOR THE RASPBERRY COULIS
250 g/9 oz/1½ cups fresh raspberries, hulled
icing (confectioners') sugar, to sweeten

1 Beat the cottage cheese and crème fraiche or natural yogurt in a bowl. Add vanilla sugar to taste.

2 Set eight perforated heart-shaped moulds on a wire rack over a roasting tin. Spoon the cheese mixture into the moulds, filling each one to the brim.

3 Transfer the roasting tin to the fridge and leave the moulds to drain for up to 2 days.

4 To make the coulis, sieve the raspberries, then sweeten with icing sugar. Turn out the moulds. Serve with the coulis, decorated with leaves.

Right: Coeur à la Crème (top); Tiramisu

Tiramisu

Rich and creamy Mascarpone makes this a wickedly indulgent and delicious dessert.

Serves 6–8

INGREDIENTS

2 eggs, separated, plus 2 egg yolks
90 g/3½ oz/7 tbsp caster (superfine) sugar
5 ml/1 tsp pure vanilla extract
500 g/1¼ lb Mascarpone
250 ml/8 fl oz/1 cup freshly brewed strong
    black coffee
60 ml/4 tbsp rum or brandy
about 24 Italian Savoiardi biscuits (cookies)
60 ml/4 tbsp finely grated dark chocolate

1 Whisk the egg yolks, sugar and vanilla in a heatproof bowl. Place over a pan of simmering water and whisk until pale and thick and the whisk leaves a clear trail on the surface. Remove the bowl and allow to cool, beating occasionally to prevent a skin forming.

2 When the mixture is cold, beat in the Mascarpone. Whisk the egg whites in a grease-free bowl to form soft peaks, then fold into the mixture.

3 Mix the coffee and rum or brandy in a bowl. Dip the biscuits quickly in the liquid, then arrange them in a glass dish. Spoon the Mascarpone mixture over the top, then sprinkle with the grated chocolate. Chill for at least an hour before serving.

Cheese & Chive Scones

Feta cheese, used here instead of butter, gives these tangy savoury scones a lovely light texture and delicious flavour.

Makes 9

INGREDIENTS
115 g/4 oz/1 cup self-raising (self-rising) flour
150 g/5 oz/1 cup self-raising (self-rising) wholemeal (whole-wheat) flour
2.5 ml/½ tsp salt
75 g/3 oz Feta cheese
15 ml/1 tbsp snipped fresh chives
150 ml/¼ pint/⅔ cup milk, plus extra for glazing
1.5 ml/¼ tsp cayenne pepper

1 Preheat the oven to 200°C/400°F/ Gas 6. Sift the two different flours and the salt into a large mixing bowl, adding any bran that has been left over from the flour in the sieve.

2 Crumble the Feta cheese and rub into the dry ingredients. Stir in the chives, then add the milk and mix to a soft dough.

3 Turn the dough out on to a floured surface and lightly knead until smooth. Roll out to a 2 cm/¾ in thickness and stamp out nine scones with a 6 cm/ 2½ in biscuit cutter.

4 Transfer the scones to a non-stick baking sheet. Brush with a little milk, then sprinkle with a light dusting of cayenne pepper.

5 Bake the scones in the oven for 15 minutes, or until golden brown. Serve warm or cold.

Cheese & Onion Herb Sticks

An extremely tasty bread which is very good with soup or salads. Use an extra-strong cheese to give plenty of flavour.

Makes 2 sticks, each serving 4–6

INGREDIENTS
300 ml/½ pint/1¼ cups warm water
5 ml/1 tsp active dried yeast
pinch of sugar
15 ml/1 tbsp sunflower oil
1 red onion, chopped
450 g/1 lb/4 cups plain (all-purpose)
  flour
5 ml/1 tsp salt
5 ml/1 tsp dry mustard powder
45 ml/3 tbsp chopped fresh herbs,
  such as thyme, parsley, marjoram
  or sage
75 g/3 oz/¾ cup grated Cheddar or
  Red Leicester cheese

3 Sift the flour, salt and mustard into a mixing bowl. Add the herbs. Set aside 30 ml/2 tbsp of the cheese. Stir the rest into the flour mixture and make a well in the centre.

4 Add the yeast and sugar mixture to the bowl with the fried onions and oil, then gradually incorporate the flour and mix to form a soft dough, adding extra water if necessary.

5 Turn the dough on to a floured surface and knead for 5 minutes until smooth and elastic. Return to the clean bowl, cover with a damp dish towel and leave in a warm place to rise for about 2 hours, until doubled in bulk. Lightly grease two baking sheets.

1 Put the water in a jug. Sprinkle the yeast on top. Add the sugar, mix well and leave for 10 minutes.

2 Heat the oil in a frying pan. Add the chopped red onion and fry, stirring occasionally, for 5 minutes, until the onion is well coloured.

6 Turn the dough on to a floured surface, knead briefly, then divide the mixture in half and roll each piece into a 30 cm/12 in long stick. Place each stick on a baking sheet and make diagonal cuts along the top.

7 Sprinkle the sticks with the reserved cheese. Cover and leave for 30 minutes until well risen. Preheat the oven to 220°C/425°F/Gas 7.

8 Bake the sticks in the oven for 25 minutes, or until they sound hollow when they are tapped underneath. Leave to cool on a wire rack.

Parma Ham & Parmesan Bread

The addition of cheese and ham makes this unusual and tasty bread extremely nourishing and filling.

Serves 8

INGREDIENTS
225 g/8 oz/2 cups self-raising (self-rising) wholemeal (whole-wheat) flour
225 g/8 oz/2 cups self-raising (self-rising) white flour
5 ml/1 tsp baking powder
5 ml/1 tsp salt
5 ml/1 tsp freshly ground black pepper
75 g/3 oz prosciutto, chopped
25 g/1 oz/2 tbsp grated Parmesan cheese
30 ml/2 tbsp chopped fresh parsley
45 ml/3 tbsp French mustard
350 ml/12 fl oz/1½ cups buttermilk
milk, to glaze

1 Preheat the oven to 200°C/400°F/ Gas 6. Flour a baking sheet. Place the wholemeal flour in a bowl and sift in the white flour, baking powder and the salt.

2 Add the pepper and the Parma ham to the bowl. Set aside about 15 ml/1 tbsp of the grated Parmesan cheese and stir the remainder into the flour and ham mixture. Stir in the chopped fresh parsley. Make a well in the centre of the mixture.

3 Mix the mustard and buttermilk in a jug, pour into the well in the centre of the flour mixture and quickly mix to a soft dough.

4 Turn the dough on to a floured surface and knead briefly. Shape into an oval loaf, brush with milk and sprinkle with the remaining cheese. Place the loaf on the prepared baking sheet.

5 Bake the loaf in the preheated oven for 25–30 minutes, or until it is golden brown. Carefully transfer it to a wire rack to cool.

Artichoke Rice Cakes
with Manchego,
16-17

Beef: Little Meatballs
with Fontina, 22-3
Rump Steak with
Roquefort & Walnut
Butter, 42-3
Bread: Bread & Cheese
Soup, 10
Cheese & Onion
Herb Sticks, 60-1
Parma Ham &
Parmesan Bread,
62-3
Brie, Grilled with
Walnuts, 12

Cannelloni with Tuna,
34-5
Cauliflower &
Gorgonzola Gratin,
30
Cheesecake, Lemon &
Lime, 52-3
Cherry & Hazelnut
Strudel, 54-5
Chicken: Chicken

Cordon Bleu, 40-1
Parmesan Chicken
Bake, 38-9
Coeur à la Crème,
56-7

Fondue, Swiss, 46-7

Gorgonzola &
Cauliflower
Gratin, 30

Haddock with Gruyère
and Leek Sauté 36-7

Leeks: Haddock with
Gruyère and Leek
Sauté 36-7
Leeks with Cheese
& Yogurt Topping,
Baked, 28-9
Lemon & Lime
Cheesecake, 52-3

Meatballs with
Fontina, 22-3
Mediterranean
Vegetables with
Halloumi, 15
Mushrooms: Wild

Mushroom Gratin
with Beaufort
Cheese, 24-5

Onion Tarts with
Goat's Cheese, 18-19

Parma Ham &
Parmesan Bread,
62-3
Parmesan Chicken
Bake, 38-9
Pears, Cheese-stuffed,
13
Pizza with Four
Cheeses, 31
Polenta Baked with
Cheese, 32-3
Potted Stilton, 14

Rice: Artichoke Rice
Cakes with
Manchego, 16-17
Risotto with Four
Cheeses, 48-9

Sausage & Cheese
Tortilla, 20-1
Scones, Cheese &

Chive, 58-9
Soufflé, Classic Cheese,
44-5
Soups, 10-11
Spinach in Filo with
Three Cheeses, 50-1
Squash & Gruyère
Soup, 11
Stilton, Potted, 14
Strudel, Cherry &
Hazelnut, 54-5
Swiss Fondue, 46-7

Tagliatelle with
Gorgonzola Sauce,
26-7
Tarts: Onion with
Goat's Cheese, 18-19
Tiramisu, 56-7
Tortilla, Spicy Sausage
& Cheese, 20-1
Tuna, Cannelloni with,
34-5
Types of Cheese, 6-8

Vegetables:
Mediterranean
Vegetables with
Halloumi, 15

This edition is published by Lorenz Books,
an imprint of Anness Publishing Ltd,
Blaby Road, Wigston, Leicestershire LE18 4SE
info@anness.com

www.lorenzbooks.com; www.annesspublishing.com

If you like the images in this book and would like to investigate
using them for publishing, promotions or advertising, please visit
our website www.practicalpictures.com for more information.

A CIP catalogue record for this book is available from
the British Library

Publisher: Joanna Lorenz
Editor: Valerie Ferguson & Helen Sudell
Series Designer: Bobbie Colgate Stone
Designer: Andrew Heath
Production Controller: Wendy Lawson

Recipes contributed by: Alex Barker, Angela Boggiano,
Carla Capalbo, Maxine Clarke, Roz Denny, Sarah Edmonds,
Silvano Franco, Carole Handslip, Christine Ingram, Sue Maggs,
Maggie Mayhew, Annie Nichols, Liz Trigg, Steven Wheeler,
Elizabeth Wolf-Cohen, Jeni Wright.

Photography: William Lingwood, Karl Adamson, Edward
Allwright, Steve Baxter, James Duncan, Michelle Garrett, John
Heseltine, Amanda Heywood, Janine Hosegood, Patrick
McLeavey, Michael Michaels, Thomas Odulate.

Cook's Notes

Bracketed terms are intended for American readers.

For all recipes, quantities are given in both metric and imperial
measures and, where appropriate, in standard cups and spoons.
Follow one set of measures, but not a mixture, because they
are not interchangeable.

Standard spoon and cup measures are level. 1 tsp = 5ml,
1 tbsp = 15ml, 1 cup = 250ml/8fl oz. Australian standard
tablespoons are 20ml. Australian readers should use 3 tsp
in place of 1 tbsp for measuring small quantities.

American pints are 16fl oz/2 cups. American readers should use
20fl oz/2.5 cups in place of 1 pint when measuring liquids.

Electric oven temperatures in this book are for conventional
ovens. When using a fan oven, the temperature will probably
need to be reduced by about 10–20°C/20–40°F. Since ovens
vary, you should check with your manufacturer's instruction
book for guidance.

Medium (US large) eggs are used unless otherwise stated.

Publisher's Note

Although the advice and information in this book are believed
to be accurate and true at the time of going to press, neither the
authors nor the publisher can accept any legal responsibility or
liability for any errors or omissions that may have been made nor
for any inaccuracies nor for any loss, harm or injury that comes
about from following instructions or advice in this book.